Lies: Half Told

Lies: Half Told

Asghar Wajahat

Translated from Hindi by
Rakhshanda Jalil

Srishti
PUBLISHERS & DISTRIBUTORS

SRISHTI PUBLISHERS & DISTRIBUTORS
64-A, Adhchini
Sri Aurobindo Marg
New Delhi 110 017
srishtipublishers@forindia.com

Copyright © Asghar Wajahat 2002

First published in 2002 by
Srishti Publishers & Distributors

ISBN 81-87075-92-9
Rs. 95.00

Cover Design by Arrt Creations
45 Nehru Apartment, Kalkaji, New Delhi 110 019
arrt@vsnl.com

Printed and bound in India by
Yugeen Printer, Noida

Contents

The Fear of Becoming Wise:
A Background

They say it is the age of mediocrity. Perhaps it is said of every age. Only those who are truly mediocre gain a lot if not everything in this day and age. But I say that it is not easy being mediocre. Had it been easy, we wouldn't live in the kind of world we do. That is, everyone would have enough to eat and cover himself with. But it isn't so, because mediocrity requires a certain basic minimum of sense and sensibility.

There is a lifelong blood-feud between art and mediocrity. When the two become friends, the artist is showered with everything a man can long for. You may well say it is a case of sour grapes. I do not know.

Like all other art forms, literature too can spot mediocrity from a hundred paces. A great poet speaks a great truth which, often times, we call untruth simply for the sake of our own convenience. Or, we belittle it by saying it is not possible.

Of all forms of public life, politics has the greatest number of successful mediocre persons because politics draws its sustenance from the sweat and blood of the common man. And, as we say in Hindi: all thieves are first cousins. So politics, or the political arena, is where I find the most grist to my mill.

I have tried to verbalise a certain truth through my stories. It is possible that I may be deluding myself and after reading my stories you will say that like all mediocre people who love to play with the word 'truth', I have trumpeted my so-called truthfulness when all else has failed. Others may think I have tried hard to reach a certain level of 'maturity' by showing things in their true perspective.

This reminds me of my two lady friends, one an Indian and the other a foreigner, who have quite made up their mind that they will refuse to grow up, to become 'mature', that is. They insist there is no conjunction whatsoever between age and maturity. This premium on so-called maturity or mature thinking is a vile conspiracy of a handful of people.

I would put it differently. I say fear wisdom. The book of compassion is deeper and far more evocative than the book of knowledge. Look for the child within you. Look at the world with a child's smiling, curious eyes. But who listens to me.

January 2002
New Delhi

ASGHAR WAJAHAT

Introduction

Much of Asghar Wajahat's writing – whether it is stage plays, television documentaries, film scripts, street theatre, novels, short stories, or anything else that may defy categorization – holds a mirror up to society. In it we see a slice of contemporary life. There is a measure of social concern and awareness that penetrates, and in a way, characterizes, his entire ouvre.

This collection of satirical sketches and essays snaps a metaphorical finger in front of our eyes. It tells us to wake up and look around before it is too late and it does so with no great vim and vigour. The hallmark of Asghar Wajahat's writing is its steadfast refusal to strike any loud notes. Each of these ten-part series carries a tiny picture of our everyday life, a cameo of our very "Indianness" an unabashed look at the life and times of an ordinary man from the eyes of an ordinary man. These are the "smelling salts" we have all been looking for – to bring us to our senses with their strong, pungent, down-to-earth aroma.

Asghar Wajahat believes in taking on any number of 'holy cows'; nothing is too sacred or too profane for him. And so we have here a take on just about everything that is integral to the modern Indian milieu: communalism, politics, politicians, fast food, civil servants, escaped lunatics, gurus and chelas, maulvis and pandits... It is a jumble and a glorious jumble at that.

The sketches and short essays that have been selected for this volume were written over a longish period of time. It was easy, however, to spot a continuity and a common concern in them and to put them together in the form of a book. A common thread binds each of the ten-part "series". They are all, uniformly, short, sharp and sassy. They are also witty, acerbic and completely unsentimental. Each of the series hangs on a "peg" and it was easy to group them as such. In fact, in many cases, the titles and sub-titles for the series virtually suggested themselves.

Asghar Wajahat's Hindi has a fluid, smooth readability. He keeps his syntax short and uncluttered. There is an economy, even an avoidance of exaggeration and embellishment. There is no rhetoric, no verbal pyrotechnics, no elaborate wordplay. In short, there is everything here that makes a translator's job that much easier.

RAKHSHANDA JALIL

ONE
Dialogue: Life, Tamasha, Revolution
"Words have no meaning."

I

Hariram: What is Man, Gurudev?

Guru: It is a type of animal, Hariram.

Hariram: What does this animal do, Gurudev?

Guru: It produces thoughts.

Hariram: What does it then do?

Guru: Then it builds a Palace of Thoughts.

Hariram: And then?

Guru: Then it roams around and ponders on them.

Hariram: Then?

Guru: Then it eats up the lot.

Hariram: And after that?

Guru: It produces new thoughts.

II

Hariram: Gurudev, what will the simple man do if he sees two hungry dogs fighting over a bone?

Guru: He will try to mediate between them.

Hariram: And what will the clever man do?

Guru: He will run off with the bone.

Hariram: And what will the politician do?

Guru: He will let loose two more hungry dogs on the scene.

III

Guru: Hariram, you must mingle with the crowd to watch the spectacle.

Hariram: Why, Gurudev?

Guru: If you can't become a part of the crowd, you will become the spectacle yourself.

IV

Guru: Your life has been ruined Hariram.

Hariram: Why, Gurudev?

Guru: You haven't been able to learn how to use your tongue.

Hariram: But I know how to use a sword, Gurudev!

Guru: A sword can slash a man's neck but a tongue can flay you alive.

V

Hariram: What is revolution, Gurudev?

Guru: Revolution is a bird, Hariram!

Hariram: Where does it live, Gurudev?

Guru: It lives on the tongues of clever men and in the hearts of simple folk.

Hariram: What do clever men do with it?

Guru: They praise it, sing paeans celebrating it and at the opportune moment, gobble it up.

Hariram : And what do the simple folk do with it?

Guru: It forever eludes them.

VI

Hariram:	What is Creation, Gurudev?
Guru:	It is a grazing ground, Hariram!
Hariram:	Who grazes there?
Guru:	Those who have eyes.
Hariram:	Who are those who have eyes, Gurudev?
Guru:	Those who have tongues.
Hariram:	Who has a tongue, Gurudev?
Guru:	Those who have intelligence.
Hariram:	Who has intelligence, Gurudev?
Guru:	Those who have a tail.
Hariram:	Who has a tail, Gurudev?
Guru:	Those who wish to have a tail.

VII

Guru: Hariram, tell me, what is the secret behind success?

Hariram: Hard work, Gurudev!

Guru: No.

Hariram: Intelligence?

Guru: No.

Hariram: Honesty?

Guru: No.

Hariram: Love?

Guru: No.

Hariram: Then what is the secret behind success, Gurudev?

Guru: Failure.

VIII

Hariram: What is the greatest spectacle of all, Gurudev?

Guru: The greatest sight to behold is a flatterer at work, Hariram.

Hariram: Why, Gurudev?

Guru: Because a bootlicker can lap up even the greatest spectacle.

IX

Hariram: What is honesty, Gurudev?

Guru: It is the name of a dreadful deadly disease.

Hariram: Is it found in our country too?

Guru: A long time ago, Hariram, there was no cure for honesty – like there was no cure for plague, T.B. and cholera. Then it was rampant in our country and took a heavy toll of our countrymen each year.

Hariram: And now, Gurudev?

Guru: Now a drug has been discovered to curb this disease.

Hariram: What is the name of that drug, Gurudev?

Guru: It is on the mouth of every lisping infant in our country – Greed.

X

Hariram: Gurudev, if a beautiful woman has two lovers fighting over her, what should she do?

Guru: Look for a third lover.

Hariram: Why, Gurudev?

Guru: Because those who fight over a woman can't be lovers.

TWO

Conversations on Communalism: "Who will be left to live peacefully ever after?"

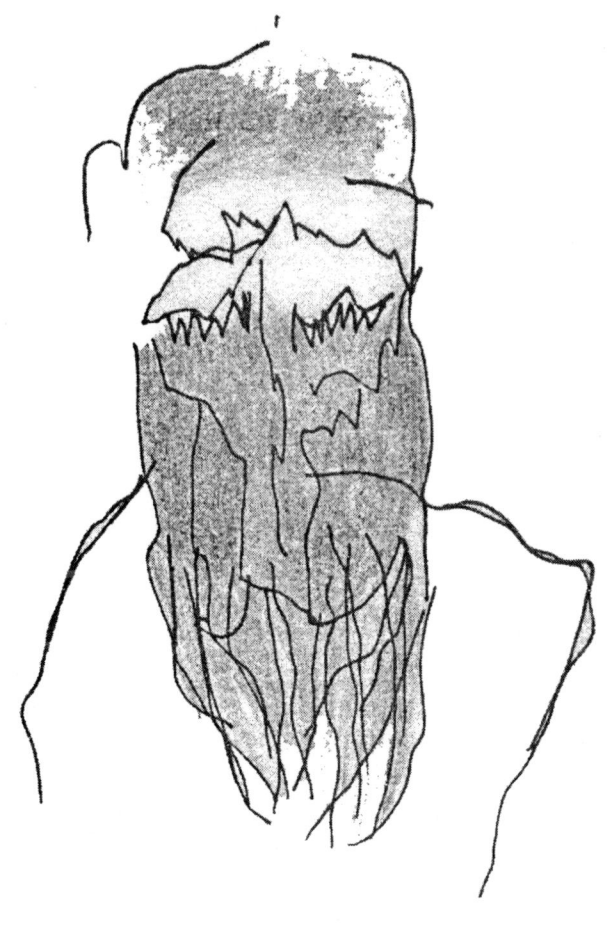

I

Hariram:	Gurudev, are the Muslims of this country outsiders?
Guru:	Yes, Hariram, they are outsiders.
Hariram:	Where did they come from?
Guru:	They came from Arabia, from Iran, from Turkestan.
Hariram:	But where do they belong now?
Guru:	They are Indian citizens now.
Hariram:	Which languages do they speak?
Guru:	Indian languages.
Hariram:	Their customs and life styles resemble the people of which lands?
Guru:	The people of India.
Hariram:	Then how are they outsiders, Gurudev?
Guru:	Because their religion is a foreign religion.
Hariram:	Where did Buddhism spring from?
Guru:	From India.
Hariram:	Then should all the Chinese, Japanese, Thai and Burmese Buddhists migrate to India?
Guru:	No, no, Hariram! What would the Chinese, Japanese, Thai and Burmese do in India?
Hariram:	Then why should the Indian Muslims go to Arabia, Iran or Turkestan?

II

Guru: Hindus and Muslims can never live together.

Hariram: Why not, Gurudev?

Guru: There are far too many differences between the two.

Hariram: Such as?

Guru: Their language is different from ours.

Hariram: Muslims don't speak Hindi, Kashmiri, Sindhi, Gujrati, Marathi, Tamil, Telugu, Oriya, Bangla, etc ... Do they only speak Urdu?

Guru: No, no, ... the difference is not of language; our religions are different.

Hariram: Do you mean people of different faiths can not live in one country?

Guru: Yes, India belongs to Hindus and Hindus alone.

Hariram: Then we must get rid of all the Sikhs, Christians, Jains, Buddhists, Parsis and Jews.

Guru: Yes, we must throw them all out.

Hariram: Then who will remain in this country?

Guru: Only Hindus shall live here ... live peacefully ever after.

Hariram: The way only Muslims live in Pakistan and live in peace.

III

Guru:	You must hate Muslims, my child.
Hariram:	Why, Gurudev?
Guru:	Because they are cruel, illiterate and dirty.
Hariram:	I understand, Gurudev. You mean one must hate cruel, illiterate and dirty people.
Guru:	No, ... no. Well, actually, one should hate the Muslims because they are extremely religious.
Hariram:	I shall hate all extremely religious people.
Guru:	No, ... no. You have not understood ... we should hate the Muslims because they once ruled over us.
Hariram:	Then we must hate the Christians too.
Guru:	No, ... no. The principal reason to hate Muslims is because they caused the partition of our country.
Hariram:	Then we must also hate those who divided our country.
Guru:	Yes, ... yes. Absolutely, we must hate those who divided our country.
Hariram:	And what should we do with those who divide our countrymen?

IV

Hariram: Gurudev, what sort of people die in communal riots?

Guru: All sorts of important religious leaders, pandits and maulvis, big-time capitalists and moneylenders, officials and bureaucrats – these are the people who get hurt in communal riots.

Hariram: And who are the people who do not get killed?

Guru: Ordinary people, workers, craftsmen, rickshawpullers, vendors, office-goers – these are the people who are never killed in riots.

Hariram: Then, Gurudev, why is it that riots still take place?

Guru: Elementary, my child, ... the ordinary man has no interest whatsoever in stopping communal riots.

Hariram: And the "big" people?

Guru: They, poor things, try their best to put an end to these riots. The pandits and maulvis give speeches to root out communalism. Politicians try their darndest to stop all riots from ever taking place. Moneylenders and capitalists give generous donations to stop rioting. Government officials too put in all they have to stop riots.

Hariram: How come the riots still don't stop?

Guru: This is the eternal mystery, my child. If ever you unravel it, you too will perish in a riot.

V

Hariram: Gurudev, why is it that the culprits behind communal riots are never punished by the Law?

Guru: That is the greatness of our system, my child.

Hariram: How, Gurudev?

Guru: Our courts understand the sentiments of those who have killed in communal riots.

Hariram: What do they understand?

Guru: Child, those who die in communal riots go straight to heaven, don't they?

Hariram: Yes, they do.

Guru: Who is responsible for sending them to heaven?

Hariram: Those who have killed them.

Guru: Absolutely correct! You see, my child, our legal system is not so utterly without shame that it will hang those who oblige others.

VI

Hariram: Gurudev, how can riots be stopped forever?

Guru: Child, the whole nation cannot answer this question for you. Not even the president or the prime minister, the entire cabinet of ministers, the intelligentsia – no one has the answer.

Hariram: Gurudev, man has reached the moon, conquered the universe, everything that was impossible till yesterday has become possible today. Why can't we entrust our scientists with the task of finding out how communal riots can be eradicated forever?

Guru: Child, scientists were put on the job but they said this was a religious issue.

Hariram: Were the religious people then put on the job?

Guru: Yes, they were, but they said this was a social issue.

Hariram: What did the sociologists have to say?

Guru: They said it was a political issue.

Hariram: So what did the politicians say?

Guru: They said it was a non-issue.

VII

Hariram: Gurudev, is the prime minister ultimately responsible
            for communal riots in this country?

Guru: No.

Hariram: The chief ministers, then?

Guru: No.

Hariram: The home minister?

Guru: No.

Hariram: Well, is it the members of parliament or legislators?

Guru: No.

Hariram: It must be the bureaucrats and police?

Guru: No.

Hariram: Then who is responsible for communal riots?

Guru: The janata.

Hariram: Meaning...?

Guru: Meaning, we are responsible.

Hariram: Meaning...?

Guru: Meaning, no one is responsible.

VIII

Hariram: Gurudev, do Muslims produce more children than others?

Guru: Yes, my child, they do nothing but make more marriages and produce more children.

Hariram: But, Gurudev, why do the Muslims have so many children?

Guru: Someone who has children of his own could tell you that... I have been an ascetic all my life.

IX

Hariram: Gurudev, are all Muslims terrorists?

Guru: Yes, my child. They do all manner of violent acts, breaking and destroying things.

Hariram: Why do they do that, Gurudev?

Guru: Because violence is in their blood, my child.

Hariram: Why is violence in their blood, Gurudev?

Guru: Must be the will of Bhagwan ji; He must have put it inside them.

Hariram: But the Muslims do not believe in Bhagwan ji; they believe in Allah.

Guru: Then it must be the will of Allah.

Hariram: But we don't believe in Allah.

Guru: Never mind, then … it must be our will.

X

Hariram: Gurudev, are all Muslims traitors?

Guru: Yes, my child, they are making our country hollow from inside.

Hariram: How, Gurudev?

Guru: They do not pay income tax.

Hariram: How, Gurudev?

Guru: Tell me, … where do you normally see Jumman?

Hariram: At the rickshaw stand.

Guru: Where do you see Bafati?

Hariram: In the crowd of daily wagers squatting beside the road.

Guru: What does Khairati do, Hariram?

Hariram: He sells blood, Gurudev.

Guru: And what does Rahmatun do?

Hariram: He makes bidis.

Guru: Now tell me, … have you ever seen them at the Income Tax Office?

Hariram: I have never been to the Income Tax Office, Gurudev.

THREE
The Mark of a Developed Country: "The eyes that see are mine, the rest belongs to them."

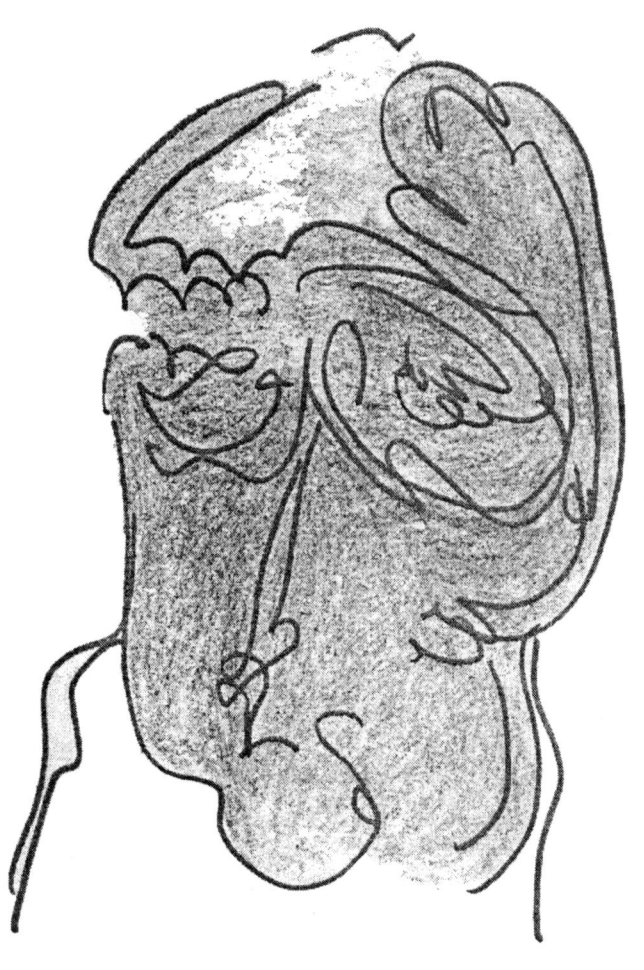

I

Guru: Tell me the mark of a developed country, Hariram.

Hariram: Developed countries do not make cloth, Gurudev.

Guru: What do they make, then?

Hariram: They make weapons.

Guru: How do they cover their nakedness?

Hariram: Their weapons cover their nudity.

II

Guru: Tell me the mark of a developed country, Hariram.

Hariram: People do not cook in a developed nation.

Guru: Then what do they eat?

Hariram: They eat "fast food".

Guru: What is the difference between "fast food" and our food?

Hariram: We approach our food whereas "faster food" gallops towards the eater.

III

Guru: Tell me the mark of a developed country, Hariram.

Hariram: Children are not born in developed countries.

Guru: Then who are born there?

Hariram: Full grown adults are born there, who start working from the moment of their birth.

IV

Guru: Tell me the mark of a developed country, Hariram.

Hariram: There is true democracy in developed countries.

Guru: How so, Hariram?

Hariram: Because they have only two political parties.

Guru: Why not a third?

Hariram: Because true democracy ends with the birth of a third political party.

V

Guru: Tell me the mark of a developed country, Hariram.

Hariram: People love animals in developed countries.

Guru: Why?

Hariram: Because animals love people.

Guru: Why don't animals love animals and people love people in such places?

Hariram: Because in developed nations people don't meet people and animals don't meet animals.

VI

Guru: Tell me the mark of a developed country, Hariram.

Hariram: Developed countries give aid to developing countries.

Guru: And then?

Hariaram: Then they give loans.

Guru: And then?

Hariram: Then loans with interest.

Guru: And then?

Hariram: Then the interest as loan.

Guru: And then?

Hariram: And then developed countries acknowledge the developing countries as developed.

VII

Guru: Tell me the mark of a developed country, Hariram.

Hariram: The elderly live on their own in developed countries.

Guru: And the young?

Hariram: They too live on their own.

Guru: And the middle aged?

Hariram: They too live on their own.

Guru: Then who lives with each other?

Hariram: Each to his own, Gurudev.

VIII

Guru: Tell me the mark of a developed country, Hariram.

Hariram: There are more mentally ill people in developed countries.

Guru: Why? Why not physically ill?

Hariram: Because they have been able to control the body, but the mind is another matter.

IX

Guru: Tell me the mark of a developed country, Hariram.

Hariram; Developed countries have a high rate of divorce.

Guru: Why is that?

Hariram: Because more people fall in love.

Guru: Why do love marriages end in divorce?

Hariram: So that one can fall in love again.

X

Guru: Tell me the mark of a developed country, Hariram.

Hariram: Developed countries are keenly aware of human rights.

Guru: Why?

Hariram: Because they possess the world's largest armed forces.

Guru: Hariram, what is the connection between armed forces and human rights?

Hariram: Gurudev, developed countries are able to protect human rights only with the might of their armed forces.

FOUR
Some More Conversations:
"When the tree is upside down and the ocean fills a pail."

I

Hariram: Gurudev, what is the greatest religious duty of a Hindu?

Guru: Breaking a mosque.

Hariram: What is the greatest religious duty of a Muslim?

Guru: Breaking a temple.

Hariram: And what is the greatest religious duty for both?

Guru: Breaking mosques and temples.

Hariram: But this way all the temples and mosques would be broken down…

Guru: That would be the greatest religious act of all.

II

Hariram: Gurudev, is Pakistan our enemy?

Guru: Yes, child, it is our enemy.

Hariram: What does Pakistan want?

Guru: It wants to destroy us.

Hariram: And what do we want, Gurudev?

Guru: We want to destroy Pakistan.

Hariram: Then we are friends, not enemies, Gurudev.

Guru: How, Hariram?

Hariram: We have the same intentions, Gurudev.

III

Hariram: Gurudev, I am worried.

Guru: Why?

Hariram: There is so much poverty in our country.

Guru: Who told you that?

Hariram: Why, Gurudev?

Guru: Those who've been saying our country is poor, became rich men a long time ago. Didn't you know?

IV

Hariram: Gurudev, what is democracy?

Guru: It comes from the root word 'demo', meaning giving demonstrations.

Hariram: What are its characteristic features, Gurudev?

Guru: They can not be described, my child.

Hariram: Why, Gurudev?

Guru: They change from one minute to the next.

V

Hariram: Gurudev, what is the right age for marriage?

Guru: What a perfectly silly question!

Hariram: Why, Gurudev?

Guru: There is no right or wrong age for marriage; you should simply not marry at all.

Hariram: Why, Gurudev?

Guru: Marriage is not something you *do*.

Hariram: Then what is it, Gurudev?

Guru: It is something you *watch*.

VI

Hariram: Gurudev, is cow slaughter a sin?

Guru: Yes, it is, my child.

Hariram: Is it also a sin to leave cows on the streets?

Guru: No, that is actually an act of great virtue.

Hariram: Why, Gurudev?

Guru: Because the ordinary man gets the opportunity to serve the cattle when they are out on the streets.

Hariram: But what about the cows that come under the wheels of cars, buses and trucks?

Guru: The drivers are directly responsible for their death.

Hariram: And what about those who leave the cows on the street?

Guru: They get their milk every evening.

VII

Hariram: Gurudev, who is an Indian?

Guru: That is a strange question. Look around you ... Can't you see Indians every where?

Hariram: I can see a beggar right there in front of me.

Guru: Forget him ... look around you. What do you see?

Hariram: I can see a rickshaw-puller.

Guru: Look the other side.

Hariram: I see a very ill person.

Guru: Do you have to look for Indians on the streets?

Hariram: Then where should I look for them, Gurudev?

Guru: Look for them in five-star hotels, in farmhouses and bungalows, in houses of parliament and legislatures and ministries ...

Hariram: You mean, the people I see out on the streets are not Indians, Gurudev?

Guru: No, they are the voters.

Hariram: You mean, they are not citizens of this country?

Guru: No, they are called voters. Once in five years, even once in two or three years these days, they go to cast their vote. Don't insult your country by calling *them* Indians.

IX

Guru: Once upon a time, a Muslim and a Hindu were both praying, but their prayers were not being answered.

Hariram: Then what happened, Gurudev?

Guru: The Muslim went to Allah and the Hindu went to his Bhagwan ji.

Hariram: Then what happened?

Guru: I'll tell you, ... but first you tell me: Can Allah and Bhagwan give the same answer?

Hariram: No, Gurudev, how can that be? If both could give the same answer, why would Hindus and Muslims be forever at each other's throat?

Guru: Now we come to the interesting part: Allah and Bhagwan actually gave the same answer.

Hariram: But how can that be?

Guru: It was so.

Hariram: What was the answer, Gurudev?

Guru: Allah and Bhagwan gave the same answer ... Both said: We cannot hear your prayers. Till you install loudspeakers in your mosques and temples We cannot hear your prayers.

X

Guru: Once upon a time, a mosque and a temple were being constructed in a certain city

Hariram: You mean, everything was in readiness for a riot, Gurudev.

Guru: Don't interrupt, child.

Hariram: Sorry, Gurudev.

Guru: The mosque's minaret soared 200 feet above the ground and the temple's spire rose even higher. And so it went on … Some of the greatest mullahs were called, so were the most revered pundits. Consultations were held. Donations were collected. Money poured in… hundreds and thousands of dollars came from abroad. The minaret and the spire rose higher and higher till one day both touched the sky.

Hariram: Then, Gurudev?

Guru: Then the pundits and mullahs climbed their respective spire and minaret. They went up to meet God. They found, to their utter astonishment, that Allah and Bhagwan were actually one and the same. They were confused. They didn't know what to do. They scratched their heads and asked: If you are one, why did you make two different religions? Do you know what God said?

Hariram: What, Gurudev?

Guru: He said: If I hadn't made two religions, how would you have known how foolish you are?

FIVE
The Revolutionary Crosses
Seventy-five:
"Lovers are not fence-sitters."

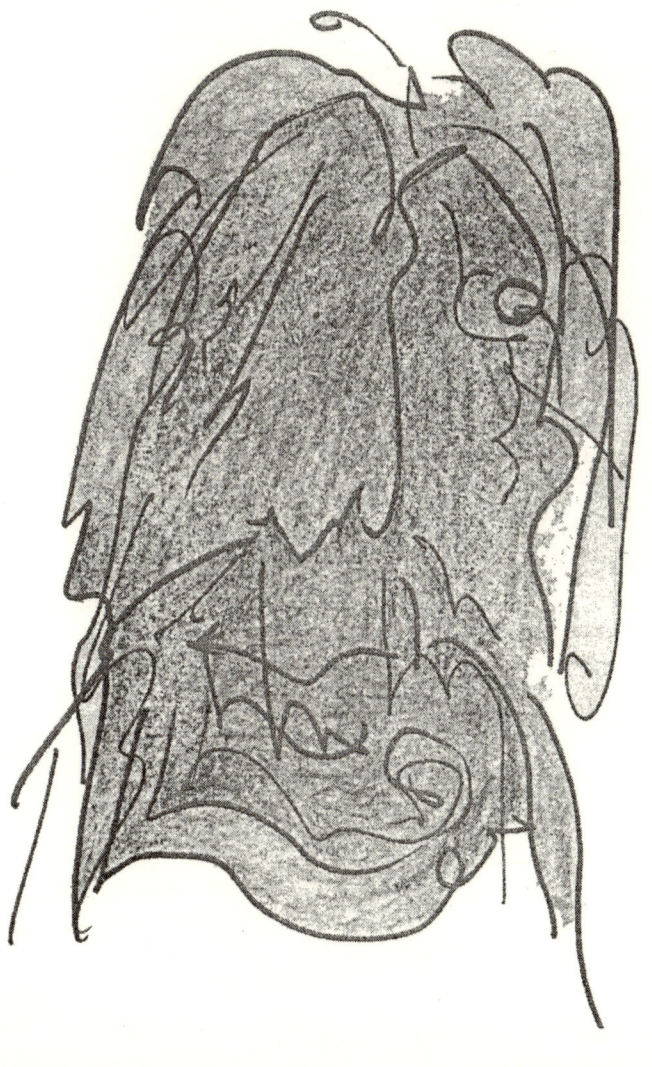

I

All his life the Revolutionary lived under the illusion that he could only use his left hand. Therefore, he never ever used his right hand even though, as everyone knows, the right hand is stronger than the left.

Now that he is over seventy-five years old, his right hand is weaker than his left.

And that is why, the Revolutionary can do everything except play the *shehnai*.

II

The Revolutionary went to a farmer and said, "Come with me, let us form a union, let us agitate. We will bring about a revolution. Everyone will get justice, everyone will have a better life."

The farmer said, "The beam of my thatched hut has broken. Come with me and help me cut a beam so that I can lay a fresh thatch over it."

The Revolutionary said, "What is this foolish talk? Here I am telling you about a revolution that will change your life and you are talking about your thatch." Saying this, the Revolutionary walked away and the farmer stood in the place of the beam to hold his thatch from collapsing.

Many years later, the Revolutionary happened to walk that way again. He saw that the farmer had turned into a beam, since he had been standing still for all those years holding up his thatch. The Revolutionary launched into a radical speech.

The farmer said, "Everything you say is true, Comrade, but I can't come with you now, even if I want to."

For a moment the Revolutionary thought of taking the farmer's arm and pulling him away, but he didn't when he thought of the thatch which would surely collapse and bury them both, if he were to do so.

III

The revolutionary got a placard made on which he wrote "Revolutionary". He hung it around his neck and set out. But no one ventured close to him.

Then he got a metal helmet made. On this, too, he wrote "Revolutionary", but still no one came up to him.

Then he got a suit of armour made, on which he wrote the entire *Das Kapital*. He wore the armour and stood up. But when he tried to walk, he found he couldn't take a single step. When he tried to sit down, he found he couldn't, neither could he talk nor laugh. He could only stand. He stood for years, his body inside the armour rotted away but the suit of armour continued to stand in its place.

IV

The Revolutionary knew English, he also knew German, French, Russian, Italian, Spanish but he knew no Hindi. Someone asked him, "How will you bring about a revolution in India when you know no Hindi?"

The Revolutionary answered, "First I will bring about a revolution in England, then in Germany, followed by France, Russia, Italy, Spain, … and when the revolution has already taken place in all these countries, we will bring about a revolution in India without knowing any Hindi."

V

All his life, the Revolutionary failed to unravel the mystery why the poor, the downtrodden, the exploited, the untouchables and the minorities never ever came to him – even though he was their true and honest sympathizer.

He went to meet the greatest leader of his party and put this question before him. The greatest leader of his Party was a decrepit old man, well over a hundred years. Even his eyelashes and eyebrows had turned white. He heard the Revolutionary's question and asked, "Does that mean our vision is wrong?"

"No, no, Comrade," the Revolutionary panicked.

"Then is the Party wrong, Comrade?"

"No, no, Comrade," cried the Revolutionary plaintively.

"Go and do your work and stop talking such nonsense."

The Revolutionary got down to work in earnest. Many years later, when he had still not found the answer to his question, he went to an astrologer and asked him the same question. The astrologer said, "Give me five rupees and twenty-five paise and I will give you the answer."

The Revolutionary placed five rupees and twenty-five paise on the man's upturned palm.

VI

One night, the Revolutionary saw Karl Marx in a dream, but strangely enough, Karl Marx was clean shaven.

The Revolutionary asked, "Lord, what have you done?"

Karl Marx replied, "I haven't done it; you people have done it to me."

VII

For a long time now the Revolutionary had not gone "underground". It began to feel strange. One night, as he lay in bed with his wife, he said to her, "Listen, Comrade, we haven't gone underground for a very long time."

The wife replied, "Don't talk and lie still ... I am very sleepy."

VIII

Fifty years ago, the Revolutionary used to chant revolution-revolution like a mantra. Morning-noon he recited it like a prayer. He could see the revolution in his dreams, but he never ever saw it in his waking moments. It made him sad. But he kept quiet for ten long years. And all that while he kept searching for a new word. After a long and arduous search, he found the new word – government.

For the next five years, the Revolutionary chanted the word "government" like a mantra and soon he found government.

Now the Revolutionary never ever breathes the word "revolution" – not even in his dreams. He is scared that if he so much as utters that wretched word, he may lose the new word.

IX

Fifty years ago the Revolutionary had kept a mountain parrot as a pet. He taught the parrot to say, "The revolution will come … the revolution will come … Don't worry, Brave Son of the Revolution."

When the Revolutionary left home in the morning and returned in the evening, the parrot would trill the rehearsed words.

One day, no one knows how, the parrot sang out, "The revolution has come … the revolution has come … don't worry, Brave Son of the Revolution."

Now the parrot lives in a gilded cage.

X

The Revolutionary has such a magnetic personality that whoever came in contact with him became a revolutionary. But the Revolutionary is dead against any form of nepotism. That is why his elder son is a businessman settled in America. The younger son has a travel agency in Mumbai. The elder daughter owns a garment factory. The younger daughter is a stakeholder in a major T.V. channel.

But the Revolutionary himself owns nothing. For the past 25 years, all he has had is a crown of thorns. And, even if the Revolutionary wants it to sit on someone else's head, the crown of thorns refuses to budge.

SIX
The Stories of Mr T. P. Dev:
The ordinariness of an ordinary man.

I

Mr T. P. Dev was an upright citizen. He kept to himself and minded his own business. Every morning he left at a quarter to eight to go to the office, and returned home at six every evening. He would drink tea, watch T.V., eat his dinner and go to sleep. Suddenly one day, no one knows why, he wondered when was the last time he had laughed. But he couldn't remember. He thought and thought, but he still couldn't remember. He looked through his papers and old diaries but found no record of such an occurrence.

He went to the doctor and told him that, as far as he could tell, he had never laughed. Was it an illness, a disease of some sort?

The doctor said, "No, this can't be an illness because there is no mention of such a disease in any of our medical textbooks." But Mr T. P. Dev was not satisfied. He consulted scores of doctors, hakims and vaids. He asked everyone the same question. Everyone gave the same answer. Mr T. P. Dev's anxiety grew.

One day Mr T.P. Dev was climbing the stairs to his apartment. He saw a young, vagabond-looking person laughing. He stared in amazement. Then he asked the boy, "Tell me, how do you laugh?"

The boy laughed harder when he heard the question.

"No, no, tell me."

The boy laughed harder still.

"Tell me, tell me," Mr T. P. Dev clutched the boy's hand in desperation.

The boy said, "Go home and look in the mirror."

Mr T. P. Dev rushed to the mirror the moment he got inside his apartment.

He saw the solemn, lugubrious face in the mirror and laughed.

II

Mr T. P. Dev had been watching television for the past 15 years. One day, when he returned to his apartment, he decided – today he would not watch television. He sat down in front of the T. V. but he did not switch it on.

Suddenly, the T. V. flickered on. Mr T. P. Dev sprang up with fright and rushed to switch it off. But it refused to switch off; in fact, it became louder. Scared witless, Mr T. P. Dev ran to another room. But the T. V. followed him there.

Now Mr. T. P. Dev ran from one room to the other, with the T. V. following close on his heels. And so the game went on.

Till, finally, Mr T. P. Dev rushed into the bathroom and bolted the door, but as he turned around, there it was – standing in front of him. He ran out again, completely drained by now and fell down on the sofa. The T. V. came and stood in front of him.

Two hands emerged from the T. V. One hand held a pill, the other a glass of water. Mr T. P. Dev swallowed the medicine and drank the water.

The T. V. switched off on its own, but Mr T. P. Dev got up and switched it on.

III

One evening Mr T. P. Dev decided to go to the park to relax. By a stroke of good fortune, he found two empty benches. Mr T. P. Dev quickly sat down on one. Then he got up and sat on the other. A few minutes later, he came back to sit on the first bench. Then he sat on one and propped his feet up on the other. Then he sat on the first and kept a proprietorial hand on the second. After a while, he joined the two benches and lay down on both. He hadn't been lying for more than a few seconds, when he got up and stood on the benches. Then he jumped off them and began to move the benches around. He climbed one and began to leap from the other.

By now the sun had set. Mr T. P. Dev returned home a happy man.

IV

One day, Mr T. P. Dev's telephone rang. He picked up the telephone. A voice on the other end said, "I am your father speaking."

Mr T. P. Dev said, "Sorry, wrong number," and put the phone down.

The phone rang again after some time. "Hello," said Mr T. P. Dev.

"This is your wife speaking."

"Wrong number," said Mr T. P. Dev and put the phone down.

The phone rang again. This time a voice said, "I am your son."

"Sorry, wrong number," and Mr T. P. Dev put the receiver down.

The phone rang again. "Hello," said Mr T. P. Dev.

"How are you?" asked a voice.

"Who is speaking?" asked Mr T. P. Dev.

"I am Mr T. P. Dev speaking," said the voice from the other end.

"Very sorry, wrong number. Don't dial this number again. This number does not belong to anyone. Do you understand?"

V

Mr T. P. Dev went to the seaside for a holiday. He stayed at a luxury beachside hotel. He got up in the morning, took a bath, wore a suit with a tie and went down to the restaurant for breakfast. He came out of the hotel and got into a waiting taxi. He told the driver, "The office of the International Finance and Investment Corporation."

The taxi moved. Mr T. P. Dev opened his newspaper and began to read.

Exactly seventeen minutes and twenty-two seconds later, the taxi deposited him in front of his office.

VI

Mr T. P. Dev saw an advertisement: "Fill your neighbour's heart with envy. Buy this car." The message struck home. Mr T. P. Dev went out and bought the car.

But he didn't know which car his neighbour had. He didn't even know who his neighbour was or where he stayed. However, he knew what envy was.

VII

Mr T. P. Dev was vehemently opposed to giving money to beggars. One day a beggar asked him for money. Mr T. P. Dev refused.

"Why do you refuse?" the beggar asked.

"Because you are a beggar and I am very against giving money to beggars," Mr T. P. Dev said and began to walk away.

The beggar chided him, "You think I am a beggar? I am the Managing Director and Chairman of a company that employs hundreds and thousands of beggars. My ambassadors live in some of the world's most prosperous countries. Every year the International Monetary Fund and the World Bank give me millions of dollars. Do you understand?"

Flustered, Mr T. P. Dev handed him his entire wallet.

VIII

Mr T. P. Dev was scared of all living things. That was why he never kept a pet dog or cat. It was his firm belief that one could never fully trust another living thing and that one should always be a little skeptical of the loyalty of another living thing.

One day, as Mr T. P. Dev lay resting peacefully, his hand wandered up to the left side of his chest. And he heard the rat-a-tat of his own beating heart. He got up with a start. What did this mean? That he was a living thing himself!

He rushed to the hospital. The sad report was that he was, indeed, alive. Now Mr T. P. Dev came to regard himself as a form of life even lower than a dog or a cat.

For the rest of his life he remained in mortal dread of the living thing lodged inside his chest. Yes, he found peace after his death.

IX

One day the unexpected happened. Mr T. P. Dev found a book. He didn't know what to do with it. Such a thing had never happened to him before. Why had it happened now? The more he thought about it, the more entangled he got.

Anyhow, now that he had found a book, what was to be done with it? He thought, let me take the book and drop it in front of an enemy's house. But then he remembered, he had no enemy. Then he thought, let me give it to a friend but the same problem raised its head. He had no friend either. Then he decided, never mind, let me just go and drop it in a trashcan. But, wait, what if someone were to see him?

Fed up with his own deliberations, he called up the police.

"Police Assistance Bureau? Emergency Service?"

"Yes?"

"I am calling from Flat No. 12, Building No. 13, Road No. 14, Area Code 15, Person No. 16. I have found a book ..."

"What did you say? A book?" an agitated voice asked. "Where? When? How? Why?"

Soon a bomb disposal squad showed up. The building was evacuated. With the utmost care and precision, the book was "disabled".

X

A day came when Mr T. P. Dev retired from work. But the very next day he was back in the office. The new man who had taken his place took him to the boss's room.

The boss said, "Mr T. P. Dev, you have retired. You must learn to relax now."

Mr T. P. Dev said, "Relax, sir? Which file are you talking about?" And he looked at the boss with utter amazement.

The boss understood that Mr T. P. Dev did not know the meaning of the word "relax". To make him understand, the boss put his head down on his table and closed his eyes.

Mr T. P. Dev looked at the boss with even greater astonishment and perplexity.

The boss did not raise his head. He did not open his eyes.

SEVEN
On Becoming an IFS:
Some notable incidents in the life of
Mr T

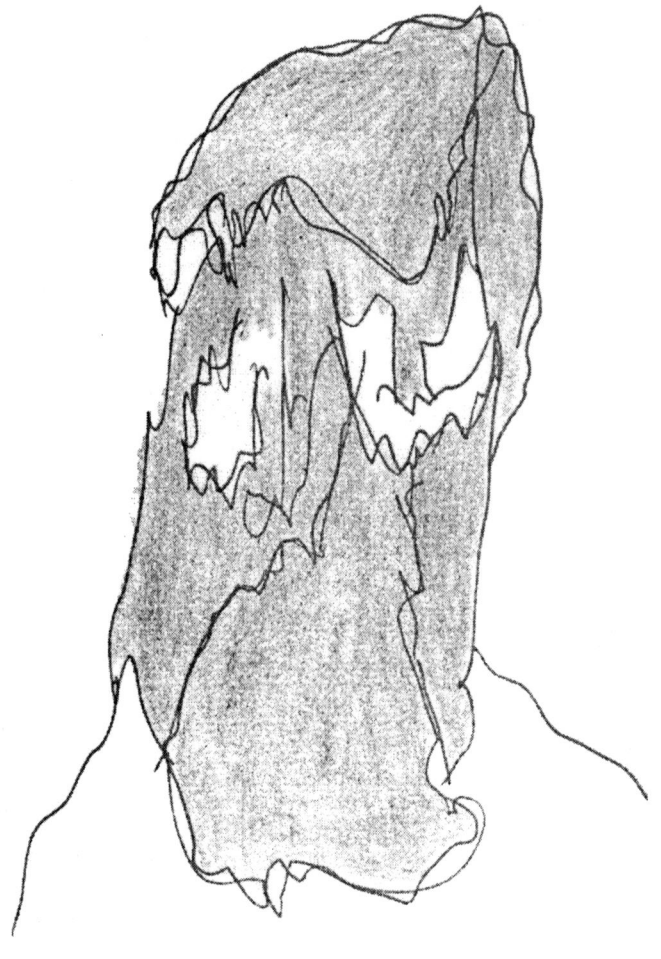

I

The year that Mr T joined the Indian Foreign Service was the same year that Miss M joined the Service. The two did not know each other. The only truly remarkable similarity between them was that both belonged to the IFS, and the biggest dissimilarity was that one was a man and the other a woman. And for this reason, they got married. Their first few postings were together, but later they were posted to different places. And so it continued till both retired. Together in their old age, they decided to have a baby. The child of old age was born old, that is, exceedingly wise. Mrs and Mr T would play with the child and his laughter would fill their hearts with delight.

It was the firm belief of both Mrs and Mr T that their child would grow up and join the IFS, marry a girl from the Service and live happily ever after – like them.

II

The Ambassador at Mr T's new posting was an untouchable. Mr T became an untouchable the moment he reached his new posting. But the Ambassador refused to believe this. Time and again, His Excellency would humiliate Mr T, sometimes under the influence of alcohol but more often than not even when stone cold sober. He began to take great delight in getting poor Mr T tied up in knots. Everyday he would try new tactics.

One day he ordered Mr T to call the Joint Secretary Mr F in Delhi and ask him about such and such matter.

Mr T bleated, "But, sir, it must be two in the night in Delhi."

The Ambassador growled, "I didn't ask you the time in New Delhi."

Mr T ventured nervously, "Joint Secretary Mr F would be sleeping at this hour, sir."

The Ambassador rounded on him with utter disdain, "I am not asking you what Joint Secretary Mr F might be doing at this hour."

Mr T stuttered, "Joint Secretary Mr F will be furious at being woken up at two in the night."

The Ambassador ordered in a tone that brooked no further argument. "Go and make that call. Don't you know that Mr F suffers from constipation?"

"No, sir."

"What sort of officer are you? Every peon at the Ministry knows this. You should know every detail of each ailment that Mr F suffers from. And also the names of all the medicines he takes for each of his ailments."

"Yes, sir," mumbled Mr T.

"Mr F had piles before he had constipation. Then he had an abscess followed by fistula. He took a posting to London to have his fistula operated upon."

"Yes, sir."

"What is this yessir yessir, … why aren't you taking notes?"

Mr T hurriedly began to take notes.

"Despite a successful operation in London, Mr F could not get rid of the constipation. When I was the First Secretary in Sofia, he had come there with a delegation. I took the utmost care in organizing his amusement and entertainment but he still complained to the Ambassador and my c.r. was blotted. Do you know what his complaint was?"

"Yes, sir."

"Then, tell me."

"Yes, sir, I mean, no, sir," squawked Mr T.

"His complaint was that I had forgotten to keep a bottle of laxative in his room."

"Yes, sir."

"I know that if Mr F is woken up in the middle of the night, he can't go back to sleep and he gets constipated in the morning. He becomes angry if he can't have a 'movement' and the angrier he gets, the more constipated he becomes. As his constipation becomes more stubborn, he becomes angrier and angrier ... Go and make that call to Mr F."

"Sir, sir, ...," Mr T whined.

"Go and call him, ... if you don't call him, I will get constipated,... if you call him, you will get constipated... Go!"

III

When the untouchable Ambassador had quite exhausted his stock of ways to make Mr T's life a misery, Mr T approached him with his sacred thread and loincloth.

"What are these, T?" the Ambassador asked.

"I am not a brahmin, sir."

"Then what are you?"

"Sir, my father came to me in a dream. He said we were never Brahmins... actually, sir, I belong to a family of untouchables."

"Do you have any proof?"

"My father came to me in a dream, sir."

"Pick up your sacred thread and loincloth, T. Go and wear them for another 200 years."

"Why, sir?"

"Haven't you heard? You can dig a dog's tail into the ground for a hundred years but it will still come out crooked ... and your tail, after all, ..."

IV

Mr T's hearing began to fail him. He could barely hear. It didn't trouble him unduly. He could now listen to the scoldings he got from the boss in the office and the wife at home to just the degree he wanted. However, years later, he wrangled a posting to the European capital, S, since it was reputed to have the best ear surgeons in the world.

Mr T got his ear operated upon, but now his eyes began to bother him. He got an operation for his eyes. Then it was the turn of his teeth to play up. He had his teeth pulled out only to discover that it had a direct effect on his brain. His mind became increasingly enfeebled. He went to his Ambassador and confided in him.

The Ambassador heard him out and said, "You should have had this operation done years ago. You haven't had very many promotions, have you?"

"Yes sir, not too many, sir."

"See, you are able to realize that only now that you have had the operation."

"Sir, if I had had the operation when I had barely joined the Service, what then?"

"Don't even think of that, T… Do you want a promotion, or not?"

V

Mr T had just popped in for a leak at the Embassy loo when he spotted his Excellency, the Ambassador, standing there. He froze at the sight of the Boss.

"Do you also pee?" asked the Ambassador.

"Sir, sir, I belong to a lowly rank."

"I asked you: Do you also pee?" the Ambassador demanded imperiously.

"Sir, sir, not like you, sir."

"What do you mean?" asked the Ambassador.

"Sir, you take a pee; I leak, sir."

"All right, then. From tomorrow onwards you shall leak at home before you come here and go home for a leak. The Embassy is no place for leaking."

The Ambassador went away in a huff. Mr T pissed in his pants.

VI

One day Mr T's Visa Officer landed him in a tight spot.

The Ambassador belonged to a royal family. His wife, the First Lady, was a royal princess. Mr T was plain Mr T.

The princess had a much-favoured gardener. In the mission's strictly hierarchical world, he enjoyed a position second only to the Ambassador. The Visa Officer had newly joined the mission. He regarded the gardener as being no better or worse than a gardener. One day, he said something to the gardener. The gardener promptly went to the princess and gave a highly embroidered version of whatever had taken place.

A phone call came from the Ambassador's residence. Mr T and the Visa Officer were summoned immediately. Mr T went, mumbling every prayer he knew.

Unfortunately, the new Visa Officer sported long hair. Mr T, too, hadn't been to the barber for several months. Getting one's hair cut was an expensive proposition in Europe and moreover, in winter it hardly mattered whether one had long or short hair bundled under a hat.

Anyhow, the two stood before the princess. She looked at the two with acute disfavour and asked: "Do you work in an embassy or are you hippies?"

"Hhhhhippy?" Mr T stuttered.

"Yes, hippy… who else has such long hair…I can't even bring

myself to look at the two of you... present yourself here tomorrow at nine sharp and make sure you have had a haircut, understand?"

The princess retreated to her personal chamber. Mr T and the Visa Officer hurried to the barber.

VII

It was one of those occasions. Mr T's wife scolded him mercilessly, and poor Mr T, … he could do nothing.

Mr T was getting dressed in a hurry to leave for the office, when his wife said, "There isn't a drop of oil in the house."

Mr T said, "I'll have a driver bring some around later."

"Make sure it comes soon; there isn't any oil to cook lunch."

Mr T reached the Embassy. He called his clerk and said, "Listen, Sharma, buy a bottle of sunflower oil and take it home."

"Sir, I'll go right away if you can arrange for a car to take me," Sharma smiled ingratiatingly.

Mr T called up the HOC who was a sharp, but arrogant, woman.

"Car? The car has gone to the airport to 'receive' His Excellency's son."

"What about the second car?" pleaded Mr T.

"The second car is taking Madam. For shopping."

"And the third car?" by now Mr T was close to tears.

"His Excellency has sent the driver of the third car to the dry cleaners."

"The fourth car."

"Fourth car? The fourth car is the 'flag car'. You know that its driver never listens to me … You will have to ask His Excellency if you want him to do something for you."

Mr T couldn't do a jot of work all day. Several urgent calls came from his home. He got a severe tongue-lashing each time. Bitter invective and endless cussing... that was his lot for the day. In the evening, a stranger came to Mr T's home carrying a bottle of oil.

VIII

One day Mr T kissed a woman in the Embassy library.

The sight of so many western beauties so enflamed Mr T's aesthetic sense that he had begun to write poetry. This business of writing poetry had a profound and dangerous effect on his personality. Its most blazing example was when he kissed the woman upon finding her alone in the Embassy library. Though the Indian Penal Code does not list kissing as a cognizable offence, nor does European sensibility regard kissing per se as offensive. Yet, for some mysterious reason, the woman chose to go to the Ambassador and complain that Mr T was presuming to equal him.

IX

There was a grand party at the Embassy. When the guests had departed, the Ambassador, quite the worse for a drink too many, summoned Mr T. Mr T thought he was being called to give an account of how much was spent on what. As he knew from long experience, every Ambassador was anxious to calculate how much was left of the allowance his country's government gave him to spend on each guest at such banquets. But when the Ambassador asked him such a deeply philosophical question, poor Mr T found himself well and truly stumped.

"After living abroad for so many years, can you live in India after retirement?"

The first requirement of Foreign Service is that when your superior officer asks you a question, you must know the answer he wants to hear from you. Mr T knew very well that the Ambassador was about to retire and that he planned to settle down in this very European capital. And with that intention, he had bought a house here which he was in the process of furnishing. Being well aware of this background, Mr T replied with perfect equanimity: "It would be very difficult, sir."

"True, true. Even if I somehow manage to live in India, what about Madam? What about the children?"

"Yes, sir ..."

"I want you to check first thing tomorrow morning which are

the items that can be 'discarded' from the residence…You know the 'rules'…"

"Yes, sir."

The next day Mr T made out a list of all those items that could be thrown out from the ambassadorial residence, such as cooking range, washing machine, air conditioner, etc. The list was so long, that save for the Ambassador, it included everything else.

X

This was His Excellency's last posting. He was planning to settle down in the capital, F. However, before he left government service, he hoped to give an unparalled gift of Indian culture and civilization to the city of F. He decided that he would open a restaurant in this capital city bustling with West European tourists.

Soon the restaurant was opened. It was named 'India'. The records showed the Ambassador's son as the owner, though everyone knew who the real owner was.

Unfortunately, the restaurant opened but the cook from India had still not shown up. As a result, the Ambassador was worried. Mr T's job was to treat the Ambassador's worries as his own worries. He said, "Sir, I belong to a family of cooks."

The Ambassador looked at him sternly. Mr T had, on previous occasions, claimed lineage with cobblers, washermen, gardeners et al. This time, however, the Ambassador chose not to venture into history; diplomacy does not demand digressions into history.

The next day, the Embassy was agog with lively debate and curiosity. Mr T was not in his office. He was busy shooting instructions to the underlings at 'India': "one kilo ground chillies"… "whole coriander"… "four kilos of sweet chutney"… "lijjat papad"…

The HOC, a clever, crooked and covetous woman, could contain

"Sir, I make great *rotis*. Yes, sir, I do, sir. Please try me and see, sir."

Soon the Embassy receptionist became the receptionist at 'India'. The Embassy guard began to stand outside 'India'. Clerks began to chop vegetables and wash meat. The Visa Officer became the bar man.

The only thing left at the Embassy was the tricolour flag. Sometimes, in the dark and silent night, it would hum to itself: *Jana Gana Mana Adhinayaka Jaya He....*

EIGHT
The Stories of an Unknown Man:
"The net is waiting to fly off."

I

He had an old black-and-white T.V. Everyone told him that the days of black-and-white were long gone; buy a colour T.V. He thought: what difference does it make?

One day the neighbour's T.V. conked off. His children came and said: "Uncle, our T.V. is not working. Can we watch a movie on yours?"

He said, "Why not."

The children came and sat down. He switched on the T.V. and the black-and-white image filled the screen. A child began to cry. Another began to scream. A third was tearing his clothes off. A fourth fainted; he'd probably had a heart attack.

He quickly switched off the television set. The unconscious child was rushed to the hospital. He was kept in the ICU where he died the next morning.

The man was arrested. A suit was filed against him. On the day of the hearing when the man came to the court, his face was awash with colour.

II

He had always used a neem twig to clean his teeth. One day he saw an advertisement exhorting him to clean his teeth with Peacock Tooth Powder. He went out and promptly bought Peacock Tooth Powder. He saw another advertisement for New Tooth Paste. The advertisement was adamant: use New Tooth Paste and nothing else for it is best for your teeth. He went and bought New Tooth Paste.

Two years later, he saw an advertisement for Ultra Refined Toothpaste. He went and bought that. Then he saw an advertisement for Galaxy Tooth Paste which categorically stated that Galaxy Tooth Paste was a bigger seller than all other tooth pastes put together. He bought Galaxy Tooth Paste. Subsequently, he saw advertisements for New Space Age and Ultra Super Space Age. He switched to those.

Then, one day, a miracle happened. He saw on the television that some of the world's greatest scientists had proved that neem twigs were by far the best way to clean your teeth. The natural goodness of neem can not be replicated in any tooth paste.

He ran to look for the nearest neem tree. But it wasn't where it used to be. Infact, he looked all over but he could not find a single neem tree. Then he went to the super market where excellent quality neem twigs could be bought – hygienically packed and far more expensive than any tooth paste. He paid for the neem twigs and came home.

He found that his teeth were now too far gone to be scrubbed with neem twigs.

III

He had deliberated long and hard before leaving Big City. When he opened his eyes on his first morning in the village, he felt liberated from the bondages of a crassly consumerist society. He took a long, deep breath. A sudden fit of coughing caught him unawares. His uncle rushed to his side and said, "Why haven't you put on your oxygen cylinder?"

"Here, too, … like Big City, you …." he tried to ask between coughing.

"You can get the cylinders quite easily in Big City; here we have to buy them in 'black'." His uncle put the inhaler close to his mouth and the coughing stopped.

"Uncle, I want to go out in the garden."

"Garden? Oh, you mean trees …son, we go to the green house in Big City when we want to see trees."

"What about mountains, Uncle?"

"They've turned into cities. The mountains were broken into little pieces, then pulverized into concrete and carted off to create cities."

"Water?"

"Don't ask about water! We get our mineral water from Big City. Here it costs fifty rupees a bottle. It must be cheaper in Big City."

"Animals, birds? What about those?"

"They are all in the Big City zoo; there's nothing to be found here now."

He was quiet for a minute or two. Then he asked, "When can I get the next bus to Big City?"

"They go every second, son."

IV

Suddenly one day, from an unknown man, he became very well known. He didn't know what to do. People would come up to meet him, flatter him, pay obeisance to him. He wanted to tell them: Look here, I am still an unknown man. But no one would listen to him

Gradually, his face began to change. He began to worry all the more. One day his face said to him: "Where will you hide now? You are no longer the unknown man."

The next day when someone caught him eating *gol gappas* from a streetside vendor, he died from sheer ignominy.

V

One day, a great leader came up to the unknown man and said, "Come with me. I will turn you into a leader of the masses."

The unknown man asked, "Why?"

The great leader said, "Because you are unknown."

The unknown man said, "But I don't want to be a leader of the masses."

The great leader said, "That is very strange. Everyone wants to be a great leader. Why don't you want to be one?"

The unknown man said, "Because I want to remain unknown."

The great leader said, "So, you want to walk alone."

The unknown man said, "Yes."

The great leader pulled out a revolver from the pocket of his starched white kurta and pumped six bullets in the unknown man's chest.

VI

The unknown man wanted to live in peace. But peace didn't want that he should live with her. The two were always at loggerheads. One day peace said to him, "Why do you dog me at every step? This is the age of terrorism and look at you – you are still chasing an old hag like me?"

He said, "I will always chase you. I like you."

She said, "Do you know what I have come to you as today?"

He asked, "What?"

"A human bomb," she said and exploded. The unknown man was blown into a million smithereens.

VII

The unknown man's heart became diseased. The doctors replaced it. His brain became diseased. The doctors changed it. Then his liver and his kidneys were afflicted. The doctors changed those too. Gradually, his eyes, nose, ears, hands, feet were replaced with new ones.

The unknown man asked, "Am I still an unknown man?"

The doctors said, "Yes, you are still unknown. However, we have become internationally famous."

VIII

The unknown man lost his walking stick. He went to the market to buy another one. He went to many shops but no one stocked walking sticks. Shopkeepers would laugh when he asked for a walking stick. Wearily, he asked one of them, "Have old people stopped walking with a walking stick?"

He was told, "They walk with a girl, not a stick!"

IX

One day, the unknown man decided that he wanted to do a good deed. He went and fetched medicine for an extremely sick woman who lived in his neighbourhood. The woman died. The unknown man was arrested. The police insisted that he sign a declaration saying he had mixed poison in the woman's medicine.

The unknown man protested, "No, I did not mix poison in her medicine."

The police said, "We don't care what you gave her, but she is dead. And you will be hanged for it. If you say you gave her poison, I can think of at least ten or fifteen people who will benefit from your declaration."

The unknown man asked, "How?"

The police said, "You see these ten or fifteen T. V. crews. They have been camping here for hours. They are hungry and thirsty. If you give a statement, they can go back, file their stories and go home."

X

The unknown man's children were always angry with him. Why was he such a nonentity, such a completely unknown man? they would ask. One day he won a lottery. He became a millionaire. Now his children had a new worry: how much of the windfall would he give and to whom. His wife began to worry because her children worried so. He worried because everyone else in his family was always worried.

Till, finally, in despair he returned the money he had won. When his children came to know about it, they were so enraged that, in a fit of fury, they killed him.

After his death, he became very well known.

NINE
Stories from the Lunatic Asylum: "The house has no doors, nor windows."

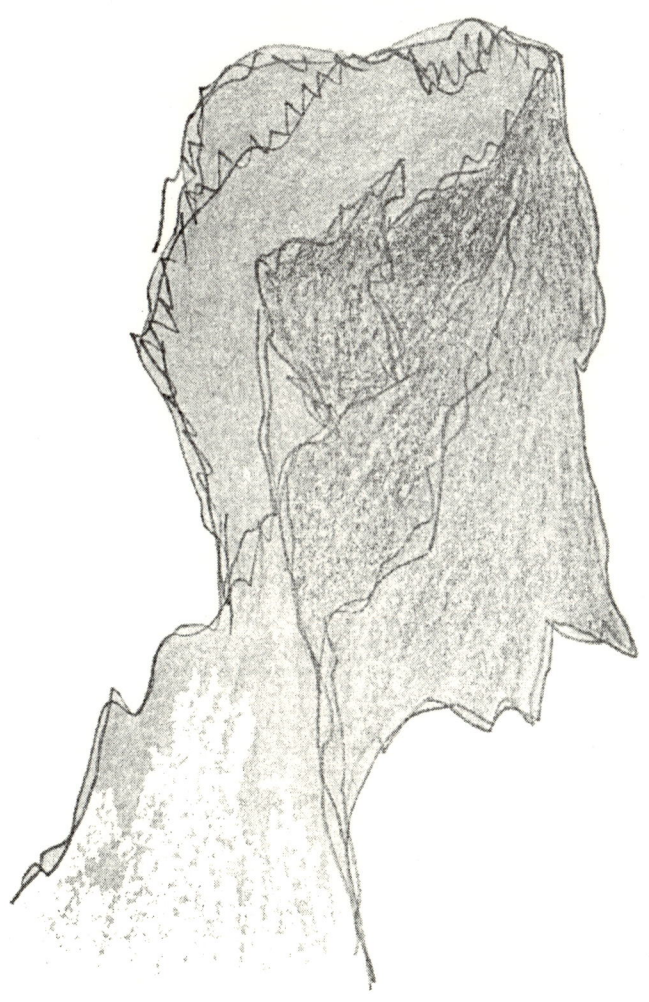

I

The day the doors of the lunatic asylum were broken down, one inmate escaped and announced that he was the President of America. Another ran away and declared he was the President of the Soviet Union. Soon, there was a scramble to see who would declare himself to be the president of where. Every inmate chose a country and declared he was the president of that nation.

But no one declared himself the President of India.

II

When the doors of the lunatic asylum were broken down, one inmate ran away and became an entrepreneur. He opened a clinic to teach people how to become mad. But no one ever came to his clinic to learn the fine art of lunacy. The clinic began to show heavy losses and the madman was close to despair. One day he set off to find out why no one ever came to his clinic. After much digging and nosing around, he discovered that there were already innumerable such clinics among the city's homes and offices.

III

When an inmate saw that the door of the lunatic asylum had been broken down, he began to cry inconsolably. He cried and cried till he made himself ill.

Some one asked him why he was crying so much. He answered: "There was only place in the entire country fit for human beings to live; that too has now been vandalized."

IV

When the doors of the lunatic asylum were being broken down,
an inmate declared loudly: "Jai Hind! Long Live India!"
Another inmate asked: "You fool, why are you saying that?"
The first inmate said: "I was locked up for saying that."

V

How did the doors of the lunatic asylum break? The government set up a 'one-man enquiry commission' comprising a retired judge to look into the matter.

The retired judge probed and enquired, looked and found out, fished and ferreted and finally tabled a report before the government. However, no one wanted to read that report. It was not even as though the report was an excessively long one. It contained, in fact, just a single sentence. But whoever read it, became mad.

VI

All hell broke loose when the leaders of the Opposition found out that the doors of the lunatic asylum had broken down and its inmates had run away and mingled with the not-mad population. And as usually happens on such occasions when the Opposition's anxiety knows no bounds, they did what they always do. They issued a statement. However, by mistake an old copy of some previous statement was issued. This dealt with their growing concern over the nation's burgeoning poverty, unemployment and deteriorating law-and-order situation. It made no mention of either madness or mad people.

Permission was sought to address this issue in the monsoon session of the parliament. Members of the ruling party strenuously opposed it, whereupon one member of the opposition smacked a gentleman from the ruling party with his brand new shoe. It was widely believed that the gentleman from the ruling party who had been smacked by the shoe was, before becoming a member of parliament, a notorious shoe-thief. He, therefore, grasped the shoe he had been hit with and began to lasciviously eye the other shoe still on the esteemed shoe-thrower's foot.

By now, the session was in bedlam. Volleys of abuse jetted back and forth. Two members of the house, one of whom was an erstwhile wrestler and the other a former smuggler, were locked in a deathly embrace. Arms and legs and fists flew in all directions. Abuse and invective filled the air. It was like a bad Hindi movie.

Everyone had joined the free-for-all punch-up.

Journalists took it all in and headed for the Press Club. They knew very well that a scene such as the one they had just witnessed would never make it to the newspapers.

Meanwhile, someone entered the parliament and announced, "Friends, the cabinet has been expanded. Your salaries have been increased. Your allowances have been doubled. You will get more pension after you leave this august assembly."

The members of parliament heard the announcement and became quiet. Peace was restored.

It was eventually discovered that the man who made the announcement had escaped from the lunatic asylum.

VII

When the doors of the lunatic asylum were broken down, one inmate ran away and began to live among sane people. Soon, it became imperative for him – and others — to find out whether he was a Hindu or a Muslim. He tried his best but failed to find out whether he was Hindu or Muslim. The leaders of the community decided it would be best to split him in half, but they soon realized that doing so would kill him. Then he would be neither Hindu nor Muslim. So they hit upon another idea – he would be a Muslim one day and Hindu the next. The day he was a Hindu, he would sweep the temple with a broom. The day that he was a Muslim, he would sweep the mosque. As a result, he never had the time to clean his own house.

VIII

When the doors of the lunatic asylum were broken down, one inmate ran away and began to live among sane people. Soon the question of his marriage was raised. Who would give his daughter to a madman? But he went ahead and put an advertisement in the matrimonial column of his local newspaper. The very next day replies poured in from girls saying they were willing to marry a madman. His neighbours were greatly perplexed. They asked one of the girls who wanted to marry him as to why she was willing to marry a madman. The girl replied that in case the madman chose to pour kerosene over her after marriage and burn her to death, at least it could be said that her husband was mad.

IX

When the doors of the lunatic asylum were broken down, one inmate ran to the University. There no one was able to recognize him for what he was. He did as he pleased and no one bothered him. One day he sat in a classroom and was easily taken for a student. Another day when he sat in the faculty staff room, he was taken for a professor. In the registrar's office, sitting in his chair, he became the registrar.

He liked the University so much that he never ever thought of running away.

X

When the doors of the lunatic asylum were broken down and the inmates ran away, those who worked there also fled. Over the years, the workers and the inmates had become such close friends and had come to resemble each other so much that it had become difficult to differentiate between the madmen and those deputed to look after them.

When one of the workers fled the asylum and reached his home, he found a madman sitting in his kitchen and his wife serving him hot *rotis* fresh from the griddle. The sight so enraged him that he pounced on the madman and beat him to a pulp. It was only then that all was revealed and it was found out who was the inmate and who the worker.